J 567.9
Dixon
Dixon, Dougal.

Meat-eating dinosaurs

MEAT-EATING DINOSAURS

by Dougal Dixon

CONTENTS

Publisher: Tim Cook
Editor: Guy Croton
Designer: Carol Davis
Production Controller: Ed Green
Production Manager: Suzy Kelly

ISBN: 978-1-84898-334-2
Library of Congress Control Number: 2010925204
Tracking number: nfp0006

North American edition copyright
© TickTock Entertainment Ltd. 2010
First published in North America in 2010 by
New Forest Press, PO Box 784, Mankato, MN 56002
www.newforestpress.com

Printed in the USA
9 8 7 6 5 4 3 2 1

Every effort has been made to trace the copyright
holders, and we apologize in advance for any
omissions. We would be pleased to insert the
appropriate acknowledgments in any subsequent
edition of this publication.

The author has asserted his right to be identified
as the author of this book in accordance with the
Copyright, Design, and Patents Act, 1988.

MEAT-EATING DINOSAURS

INTRODUCTION

Just look at it! Reaching out toward you with a mouth big enough to swallow you whole. Teeth that will grip you and shear your flesh. Jaws strong enough to crush your bones. Towering to twice your height at its hips. Powerful hind legs that can run you down wherever you flee. The greatest killing machine of all time!

But now look at this. No bigger than a chicken. Covered with down. Scampering about on little feet, darting at insects, and fleeing lizards.

Or in the middle, a wolf-sized animal. Wicked killer claw on the hind foot. Tail long and stiff as a tightrope-walker's balancing pole. Hunting in a pack. Focussed enough to leap on its prey and slash it to death.

Yes! These are the carnivorous dinosaurs. They came in all sizes and lifestyles, and were the fiercest hunters of the time. But don't worry! They are no threat to you. The last one died out 65 million years ago.

The carnivorous dinosaurs, technically referred to as the theropods, were the first dinosaurs to evolve, appearing in the second half of the Triassic period, 230 million years ago. Back in those days they preyed upon the other animals that lived at the time. Then, when the plant-eating dinosaurs evolved, they developed into different forms that were able to hunt these. It has always been like that. If ever some kind of a food source appears, then soon something will evolve to eat it. Where there are leaf-eating deer we get wolves, where grazing zebras live we get lions, and so on. When the plant-eating dinosaurs appeared and developed into lots of different shapes, then the meat-eating dinosaurs evolved all sorts of shapes as well, to be able to hunt and eat each of these.

Yet, for all their great variety in size and hunting strategies, the carnivorous dinosaurs all tended to have the same shape. If you ever came across a two-footed dinosaur that you did not recognize, you could easily tell if it was a meat eater or a plant eater. Both types walked on two legs, with the head held out at the front and balanced by a heavy tail at the back. But that is where the resemblance ended. A meat eater had a slim, lithe, active-looking body, while a plant eater had a deep body holding a voluminous stomach—digesting plants takes a much more sophisticated digestive system than digesting meat. A meat eater had long jaws and sharp teeth, while a plant eater had shorter jaws, and usually had a food-gathering beak at the front and cheeks that held the plant food while it was being chewed. Then there were the forelimbs. Meat eaters usually had three fingers or less, and these were equipped with big flesh-tearing talons, while two-footed plant-eaters had four or five fingers on the hand. The colors would have been different also. We do not know what colors they were, but comparing them with today's animals, we can guess that their color schemes would be very different. Perhaps meat eaters may have been brightly colored, striped, or spotted, while plant eaters may have had more subdued colors or even camouflage, allowing them to blend into the background.

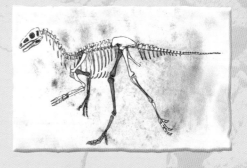

However, within this basic shape there were great variations. In size, as we have already seen, they ranged from the size of a chicken to the size of a truck. Because they ate different types of meat they had different types of teeth in their long jaws—broad blade-like teeth for shearing flesh in the big hunters, tightly packed pointed teeth for the fish eaters, and long narrow flexible jaws with little teeth for the insect eaters. Their claws evolved as a variety of different tools as well, from big curved meat-rippers, through fish-catching hooks, to sturdy digging implements that could have torn open termite nests.

We think that we, human beings, are the most successful species on the Earth. The dinosaurs we regard as ancient failures, just because they are not around any more. But we have only been here for a few hundred thousand years or so. Compare this with the history of the dinosaurs, and the carnivorous dinosaurs in particular. 165 million years as the most powerful predators on the planet!

Hardly a record of failure!

WHERE DID THEY COME FROM?

Dinosaurs! The most famous of all extinct animals, these reptiles, most of them whale-sized, dominated Earth for about 160 million years. Reptiles evolved during the Carboniferous Period, about 350 million years ago, and flourished in the succeeding Permian, Triassic, Jurassic, and Cretaceous periods. During this time, there were land-living reptiles, swimming reptiles, flying reptiles, herbivores (plant eaters), carnivores (meat eaters), and omnivores (both plant and meat eaters) — reptiles of all kinds in every environment. The age of reptiles was well under way before the first dinosaurs appeared around the end of the Triassic Period, about 225 million years ago. At the end of the Cretaceous Period, about 65 million years ago, all the big reptiles died out, and mammals took over.

EORAPTOR SKULL

An x-ray photograph of *Eoraptor*'s skull shows how its lightweight skull was made up of thin struts of bone. The dinosaur's light bone structure enabled it to move fast. The skulls of most subsequent meat-eating dinosaurs were built like this.

RAUISUCHIAN

Before the dinosaurs came along, the biggest of the hunters was a group of land-living crocodile relatives called rauisuchians. They had big heads and many sharp teeth, and, although they were slow-moving, they were faster than the plant-eating reptiles that abounded at the time.

POWERFUL LEGS

Herrerasaurus, a meat-eating dinosaur, walked on strong hind legs with its teeth and the claws on its arms held out in front, where they could do the most damage. Herrerasaurus's back was held horizontally, and the body was balanced by a long tail. This structure became the pattern for all meat-eating dinosaurs.

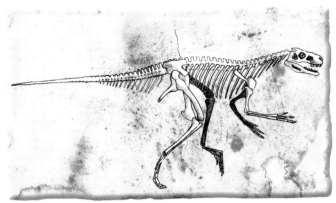

EORAPTOR

Eoraptor was about the size of a fox and, like all the dinosaurs to follow, walked on legs that were held straight under its body. This structure made it a much faster animal than the other reptiles that walked on legs sprawled out to the side.

BEFORE THE DINOSAURS

During the Permian Period, the main plant-eating animals of the time were mammal-like reptiles. They had teeth like mammals, and some were even hairy. The biggest, such as the broad-headed *Moschops*, shown here, were built like hippopotami. At about the same time as the first dinosaurs evolved, the first mammals evolved, too. Descended from the mammal-like reptiles, they were small and furry and bore live young. If the dinosaurs had not come to prominence, the mammals might have taken over. Instead, they had to wait 160 million years before evolving into more successful species.

TIGER-SIZED

Herrerasaurus was about the size of a tiger and thus was a much bigger animal than *Eoraptor*. One of the first dinosaurs, it was a primitive theropod, part of the group that includes all the meat eaters. Adults could reach a length of 10 feet (3 m). The skeleton of a *Herrerasaurus* was found in Argentina, in South America.

CARBONIFEROUS 354-290 MYA	PERMIAN 290-248 MYA	TRIASSIC 248-206 MYA	EARLY/MID JURASSIC 206-159 MYA	LATE JURASSIC 159-144 MYA

THE FIRST KNOWN

Since civilization began, people have known about giant bones embedded in rocks. In earliest times they were spoken of in legends as the bones of giants and dragons and other mythical creatures. By the early 19th century, however, scientific knowledge had advanced sufficiently for scientists to appreciate the true nature of fossils. In 1842, the British anatomist, Sir Richard Owen, invented the term "dinosauria" (terrible lizards) to classify three fossil animals whose skeletons had been discovered in England during the previous two decades. One was the plant-eating *Iguanodon*, which is now quite well known. Another was the armored *Hylaeosaurus*, which we still know very little about. The first of the trio to be brought to light and described was the carnivorous *Megalosaurus*.

FIRST DINOSAUR THEME PARK

Because of the great public interest in science in the mid-19th century, part of Crystal Palace park in South London was developed as an ancient landscape. Statues (which still stand today) were erected showing the three dinosaurs and the marine reptiles that were known at the time. All that was known of *Megalosaurus* was its jawbone, teeth, and a few fragments of bone. Since nobody knew what the animal actually looked like, it was modeled as a fearsome, four-footed, dragonlike creature.

MODERN VIEW

Even today, we do not have a clear idea of what *Megalosaurus* looked like because so few fossilized remains have been found. Like all meat-eating dinosaurs, it must have walked on its hind legs with its big head held well forward, balanced by a heavy tail. Fossils found in lagoon deposits in what is now Normandy in northern France suggest that *Megalosaurus* was a shoreline scavenger that prowled the beach, eating dead things that had been washed up.

MEGALOSAURUS JAW

The lower jawbone and teeth of *Megalosaurus* were the first parts of the animal to be discovered. They were found in Oxfordshire, England, in about 1815. The Reverend William Buckland studied them and deduced from the sharp, pointed teeth that they had belonged to a meat-eating animal and that it had been a large reptile. Other scientists studied the remains in the 1820s and one of them—history does not tell us who—came up with the name *Megalosaurus*.

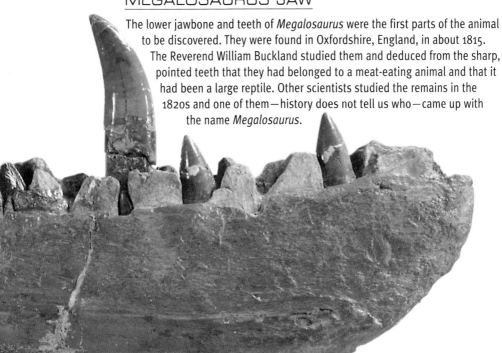

LIKE MEGALOSAURUS?

For a long time, the name *Megalosaurus* was applied to the fossil of any meat-eating dinosaur found in Britain or Europe. All kinds of unrelated dinosaurs were erroneously given the name. Only now is this mixture of different animals being sorted out. One of the dinosaurs once thought to be a *Megalosaurus* is a virtually complete skeleton of *Eustreptospondylus* in the Oxford University Museum in England.

WILLIAM BUCKLAND
(1784-1856)

This 19th-century clergyman was typical of his time. When not in the pulpit, he spent his extensive spare time doing scientific research. Most of the fossils he studied were of sea-living animals— seashells and marine reptiles. Fossils of land-living animals have always been more rare (see page 34). He may not have invented the name *Megalosaurus*, but he was the scholar who did all the scientific work on it.

TRIASSIC	EARLY/MID JURASSIC	LATE JURASSIC	EARLY CRETACEOUS	LATE CRETACEOUS
248-206 MYA	206-159 MYA	159-144 MYA	144-97 MYA	97-65 MYA

EARLY HUNTERS

Most early meat-eating dinosaurs were small, some no bigger than our cats and dogs. They probably fed mainly on even smaller animals, such as lizards and early mammals. However, most plant-eating reptiles of the time were large animals and would also have made good prey for meat eaters. Some of the early dinosaurs adopted a strategy of hunting in packs so they could bring down and kill some of these big plant eaters. Today, such teamwork is still used in the wild by animals such as Canadian wolves, which hunt moose bigger than themselves. Similarly, on the African plains, groups of hyenas attack wildebeest that are far bigger than they are.

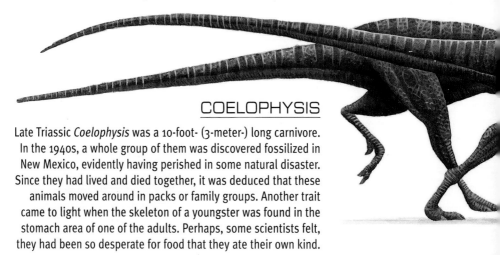

COELOPHYSIS

Late Triassic *Coelophysis* was a 10-foot- (3-meter-) long carnivore. In the 1940s, a whole group of them was discovered fossilized in New Mexico, evidently having perished in some natural disaster. Since they had lived and died together, it was deduced that these animals moved around in packs or family groups. Another trait came to light when the skeleton of a youngster was found in the stomach area of one of the adults. Perhaps, some scientists felt, they had been so desperate for food that they ate their own kind.

ONE WORLD

In Late Triassic and Early Jurassic times, Earth was very different from the way it is today. All the continental landmasses were joined together in one area, called Pangaea. Since there was only one landmass, animals of the same kind were able to migrate everywhere. This is why we find the remains of almost identical animals in New Mexico and in Connecticut, as well as in Zimbabwe, thousands of miles away on the African continent.

TRIASSIC	EARLY/MID JURASSIC	LATE JURASSIC	EARLY CRETACEOUS	LATE CRETACEOUS
248-206 MYA	206-159 MYA	159-144 MYA	144-97 MYA	97-65 MYA

BIRD & DINOSAUR FOOTPRINTS

Birds and dinosaurs are so closely related it is little wonder the footprints of one could be mistaken for those of the other. In a series of ridges of Jurassic and Cretaceous rocks in the flanks of the Rocky Mountains west of Denver, there are fossilized footprints of both dinosaurs and birds. Bird footprints can be distinguished from dinosaur prints by the greater spread of their toes—about 90° as opposed to about 45°. There is also often a trace of the little fourth toe pointing backward. In dinosaurs, this toe is usually well clear of the ground.

DINOSAUR

BIRD

SYNTARSUS

In 1972, a remarkable deposit of fossils was found in Rhodesia (now Zimbabwe). A mass of bones lay in fine river sediment, sandwiched between rocks formed from sand dunes. The fossils were of a pack of small, meat-eating dinosaurs of different sizes and ages. They seemed to have drowned in a flash flood that struck as they were crossing a dry river bed. These meat-eating dinosaurs, named *Syntarsus*, were almost identical in build to *Coelophysis,* and some scientists believe they were a species of the same animal.

THE CONNECTICUT FOOTPRINTS

At the beginning of the 19th century, long before anybody knew anything about dinosaurs, farmers in New England kept finding three-toed trackways in Triassic sandstone at the foot of the Appalachian Mountains, shown above. At first it was believed the footprints were made by giant birds that existed in the area before Noah's flood, as described in the Bible. We now know they were footprints of dinosaur packs, probably made by *Coelophysis* or something that resembled *Coelophysis*.

11

CREST-HEADED BEASTS

Look at the bright colors of many birds—the long tail feathers of a peacock, the gaudy bill of a toucan, the red breast of a robin. Color is part of a bird's method of communication. A bird's brain can "read" the colors it sees, enabling the bird to recognize whether another bird is a friend or foe. Birds are related to dinosaurs (see pages 20–21), which had similar brains and senses. It is very likely that dinosaurs also used color for communication. Some dinosaurs (especially among the carnivores) had crests and horns as brightly colored as the plumage of modern birds.

DILOPHOSAURUS IN LIFE

When it was alive, *Dilophosaurus* probably looked dazzling. Its crests may have been particularly colorful to frighten rivals or attract a mate from far away. The rest of the animal, including its dewlaps (flaps of skin beneath the chin), may also have been brightly colored to back up the signals given by the crests.

MONOLOPHOSAURUS

The crest of *Monolophosaurus*, a medium-sized, Middle Jurassic, meat-eating dinosaur from China, was made up of a pair of skull bones fused together and growing upward. Air gaps and channels between the bones were connected to the nostrils and may have amplified grunts and roars generated in the animal's throat. In this way the crest would have helped it to communicate.

HORNED MONSTER

In the Late Jurassic, one of the fiercest dinosaurs, *Ceratosaurus*, lived in North America and Tanzania. It had a heavy head with a horn on the nose and two horns above the eyes. The heavy skull suggests they may have fought by head butting, but the horns were lightly built and would not have been much use as weapons.

DILOPHOSAURUS SKELETON

Dilophosaurus was a bear-sized, meat-eating dinosaur from Early Jurassic North America. The first skeleton found had semicircular plate-like structures lying near it. Later finds showed that these structures were crests that ran parallel to one another along the length of the skull. However, what no skeleton can ever tell us is what color the crests were in life.

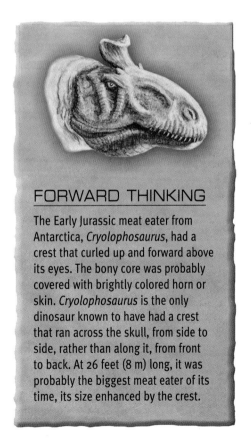

FORWARD THINKING

The Early Jurassic meat eater from Antarctica, *Cryolophosaurus*, had a crest that curled up and forward above its eyes. The bony core was probably covered with brightly colored horn or skin. *Cryolophosaurus* is the only dinosaur known to have had a crest that ran across the skull, from side to side, rather than along it, from front to back. At 26 feet (8 m) long, it was probably the biggest meat eater of its time, its size enhanced by the crest.

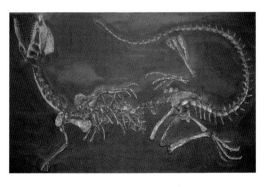

| TRIASSIC 248-206 MYA | EARLY/MID JURASSIC 206-159 MYA | LATE JURASSIC 159-144 MYA | EARLY CRETACEOUS 144-97 MYA | LATE CRETACEOUS 97-65 MYA |

SPINOSAURIDS
THE FISH EATERS

We normally think of fish-eating animals as creatures that live in the water. However, there are many land-living animals that like to eat fish, too. Grizzly bears are often seen beside waterfalls hooking out migrating salmon as they leap to their spawning grounds, and otters live mostly on land but hunt fish. It was the same in the Jurassic Period. One particular family of land-dwelling dinosaurs—the spinosaurids—seems to have been particularly well equipped for fishing. They had long jaws with many small teeth and a big claw on each hand. They lived in Early Cretaceous times, and their remains have been found across the world, from southern England to North Africa and South America.

SPINY CUSTOMER

Spinosaurus was excavated in Egypt in 1915. Unfortunately, the remains were destroyed when its museum in Germany was bombed in World War II. What we do know about it was that it was as big as *Tyrannosaurus* and had a fin down its back almost 6.5 feet (2 m) tall. The fin was probably used to cool the animal in hot weather. In 1999, a U.S. expedition found its original quarry in Egypt, so there may be hope of finding new specimens.

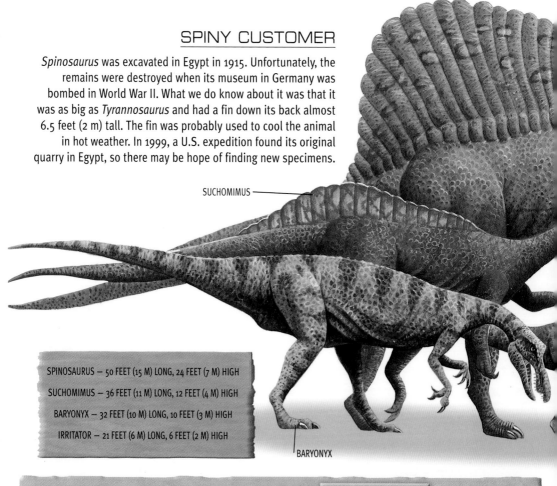

SUCHOMIMUS

BARYONYX

SPINOSAURUS — 50 FEET (15 M) LONG, 24 FEET (7 M) HIGH

SUCHOMIMUS — 36 FEET (11 M) LONG, 12 FEET (4 M) HIGH

BARYONYX — 32 FEET (10 M) LONG, 10 FEET (3 M) HIGH

IRRITATOR — 21 FEET (6 M) LONG, 6 FEET (2 M) HIGH

TRIASSIC 248-206 MYA	EARLY/MID JURASSIC 206-159 MYA	LATE JURASSIC 159-144 MYA	EARLY CRETACEOUS 144-97 MYA	LATE CRETACEOUS 97-65 MYA

HEAVY CLAW

Baryonyx was discovered by an amateur fossil collector in southern England in 1983. The skeleton was so complete that it gave us the first clear view of what these animals looked like. *Baryonyx* was an unusual meat-eating dinosaur that had crocodile-like jaws packed with sharp teeth and long forelimbs with hooked claws, which were used to catch fish.

> BARYONYX STOOD 10 FEET (3 M) TALL, AND EACH OF ITS CLAWS MEASURED NEARLY 1 FOOT (35 CENTIMETERS) LONG. WE THINK THAT IT RANGED OVER A LARGE AREA STRETCHING FROM ENGLAND TO NORTH AFRICA.

MENACING MIMIC

Suchomimus was found in a remote dune-covered area of the Sahara in 1998 by a team from the United States and Niger. A huge predatory dinosaur with a skull like a crocodile's and huge thumb claws, it measured 36 feet (11 m) long and 12 feet (4 m) high at the hip. The thumb claws and powerful forelimbs were used to snare prey, and the thin sail along its back, which reached a height of 2 feet (0.5 m) over the hips, may have been brightly colored for display.

SPINOSAURUS

AN IRRITATING EXAMPLE

Irritator was given its name because of the confusing circumstances in which it was found. The skull—all that we have of the animal—was collected in Brazil sometime in the 1990s and sent to the museum in Stuttgart, Germany. But then the museum staff had a surprise. Whoever dug it up and sold it to the museum had added pieces to it and stuck it together with car body filler to make it look much more spectacular. Now that we have had a good look at it, we can tell that it is a small spinosaurid.

IRRITATOR

BIG BITE

Many modern reptiles have features that are similar to those of the spinosaurids. Crocodiles and alligators, for example, have long jaws and many teeth, and they hunt for fish in a similar way. Like the spinosaurids, they were for a long time wrongly suspected of eating their young.

THE SMALLEST DINOSAURS

When we think of dinosaurs (a name that comes from words meaning "monstrous lizards" or "terrifying lizards"), we usually visualize the huge, fierce animals that have captured our imagination. Some dinosaurs, however, were actually not much bigger than a chicken. Scuttling around among the giants, small dinosaurs were probably more common than big ones. Unfortunately, as their skeletons were so delicate, few have been preserved as fossils. And yet, some good specimens have been found, many preserved in detail.

COMPSOGNATHUS

Compsognathus is the smallest complete dinosaur known. Although it was 35 inches (90 cm) long, most of its length was in its neck and very long tail. Alive, it would have weighed just over 5 pounds (2 kilograms), about the same as a chicken. It lived in Europe in the late Jurassic Period and must have been an active hunter.

NQWEBASAURUS

Scientists became very excited in the late 1990s when they found the almost complete skeleton of a 3-foot- (1-m-) long Nqwebasaurus embedded in Lower Cretaceous rocks in South Africa. It proved that the family to which most of the small meat-eating dinosaurs belonged (the coelurosaurids) had existed in the southern continents during the Cretaceous period, as well as in North America, Europe, and Asia.

COMPSOGNATHUS SKELETON

Two *Compsognathus* skeletons have been found: one in France, the other in Germany. The German specimen, which was well preserved in limestone, displays the skeleton and contents of its stomach, showing that its last meal included a small lizard. Some scientists thought *Compsognathus* was the baby of some other dinosaur, but the blobs scattered around the skeleton are probably eggs, proving that this was an adult.

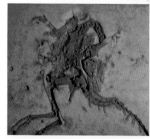

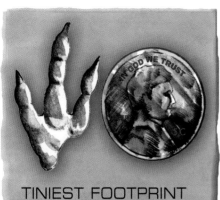

TINIEST FOOTPRINT

In the 1970s, the tiny footprint of a dinosaur that could have been no bigger than a thrush was found in the Upper Triassic rocks of Newfoundland in Canada. The arrangement of the toes is typical of the meat-eating dinosaurs of the Triassic. The print is the only trace we have of the smallest dinosaur ever found. Whether it was a youngster or fully grown, nobody yet knows.

ITALIAN BEAUTY

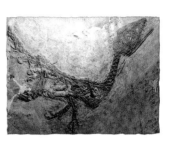

In the 1990s, this beautifully preserved skeleton of *Scipionyx* was found in Lower Cretaceous rocks in Italy. It was so finely fossilized that even some of the soft anatomy (the lungs and intestines) were preserved. Their existence confirms that this animal, probably along with all other small dinosaurs, was able to breathe efficiently while running. This would have made it an energetic and active hunter. The way the bones were articulated indicates that this specimen of *Scipionyx*, only 10 inches (25 cm) long, was not yet fully grown.

TRIASSIC 248-206 MYA	EARLY/MID JURASSIC 206-159 MYA	LATE JURASSIC 159-144 MYA	EARLY CRETACEOUS 144-97 MYA	LATE CRETACEOUS 97-65 MYA

JURASSIC GIANT

S ome dinosaurs really did live up to their reputation of being enormous, fearsome beasts. Probably the most terrifying animal of the Late Jurassic Period was *Allosaurus*. Its remains have been found in the rocks known as the Morrison Formation, which stretches down the western United States from the Canadian border to New Mexico. These deposits yielded the most important dinosaur discoveries made in the second half of the 19th century. Over a hundred different kinds of dinosaur (mostly plant eaters) were found there. The most powerful of the meat eaters found was *Allosaurus*.

FOREARMS

Allosaurus's hands had three claws: one claw, at 10 inches (25 cm) long, was much larger than the other two. The joint on this first finger allowed the huge claw to turn inward. *Allosaurus* would have been able to grasp its prey, kill it, then rip it apart. The span of its hand would have been wide enough to grasp the head of an adult man, had there been such a person around in Jurassic times!

SKULL

A typical *Allosaurus* skull is about 3.5 feet (1 m) long. The jaws were armed with more than 70 teeth, some measuring 3 inches (8 cm). The teeth were curved, pointed, and serrated, ideal for ripping the flesh of large plant-eating dinosaurs. The joints between the skull bones would have allowed the snout to move up and down to help manipulate food. The lower jaws were hinged so they could expand sideways to allow the animal to gulp down big chunks of meat.

MUSCLES

By studying the arrangement of bones in the skeleton and seeing the points of attachment for individual muscles, scientists have figured out what a living *Allosaurus* would have looked like. The leg muscles would have allowed it to move at speeds of up to 18 miles (30 km) per hour—not particularly swift but fast enough to catch the slow-moving herbivores of the time. The neck muscles would have been massive to control the huge head and powerful jaws.

TRIASSIC 248-206 MYA	EARLY/MID JURASSIC 206-159 MYA	LATE JURASSIC 159-144 MYA	EARLY CRETACEOUS 144-97 MYA	LATE CRETACEOUS 97-65 MYA

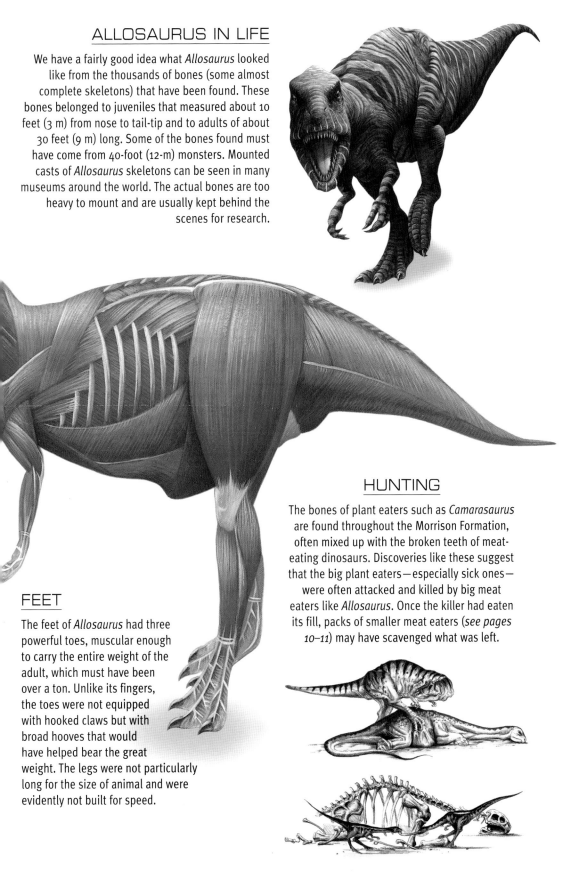

ALLOSAURUS IN LIFE

We have a fairly good idea what *Allosaurus* looked like from the thousands of bones (some almost complete skeletons) that have been found. These bones belonged to juveniles that measured about 10 feet (3 m) from nose to tail-tip and to adults of about 30 feet (9 m) long. Some of the bones found must have come from 40-foot (12-m) monsters. Mounted casts of *Allosaurus* skeletons can be seen in many museums around the world. The actual bones are too heavy to mount and are usually kept behind the scenes for research.

HUNTING

The bones of plant eaters such as *Camarasaurus* are found throughout the Morrison Formation, often mixed up with the broken teeth of meat-eating dinosaurs. Discoveries like these suggest that the big plant eaters—especially sick ones— were often attacked and killed by big meat eaters like *Allosaurus*. Once the killer had eaten its fill, packs of smaller meat eaters (*see pages 10–11*) may have scavenged what was left.

FEET

The feet of *Allosaurus* had three powerful toes, muscular enough to carry the entire weight of the adult, which must have been over a ton. Unlike its fingers, the toes were not equipped with hooked claws but with broad hooves that would have helped bear the great weight. The legs were not particularly long for the size of animal and were evidently not built for speed.

FAST HUNTERS

Back in the late 1800s and early 1900s, scientists developed a theory that birds and dinosaurs were related. This theory fell out of favor for a long time but was revived in the 1960s when a group of dinosaurs, extremely birdlike in their build, was discovered. They ranged from the size of a goose to the size of a tiger and had winglike joints in their forearms. They also had strong hind legs with huge, sickle-like killing claws on their feet, showing that they were fast runners and fierce hunters. These dinosaurs are known as the dromaeosaurids (part of a larger group called maniraptorans) and are commonly referred to as "raptors."

EARLY BIRD

This fossil of the first bird *Archaeopteryx*, dating from the Late Jurassic, was found in Germany in 1877. If it had not been for the fossil's feather impressions, the skeleton would have been mistaken for that of a dinosaur because it has a toothed jaw, clawed hands, and a long tail. As well as evolving into modern birds, some of *Archaeopteryx's* descendants may have lost their powers of flight and developed into meat-eating dromaeosaurids.

BIRD OR DROMAEOSAURID?

Right down to the killing claw on its foot, *Rahonavis*, an Early Cretaceous bird from Madagascar, had the skeleton of a dromaeosaurid. If it had not been for the functional wings, it would have been grouped with the dromaeosaurids.

TRIASSIC 248-206 MYA	EARLY/MID JURASSIC 206-159 MYA	LATE JURASSIC 159-144 MYA	EARLY CRETACEOUS 144-97 MYA	LATE CRETACEOUS 97-65 MYA

TERRIBLE CLAWS

The skeleton of a plant-eating *Tenontosaurus*, found in Lower Cretaceous rocks in Montana, was surrounded by the remains of several *Deinonychus*. *Deinonychus* probably hunted in packs, surrounded its prey, and slashed it to death. *Deinonychus* could have stood on one foot and slashed with the other, or it may have hung onto its prey with its clawed hands and slashed away with both hind feet, as cats do.

BAMBIRAPTOR

Any doubts about whether dromaeosaurids were related to birds were finally put to rest in the late 1990s, when an almost complete skeleton of *Bambiraptor* was discovered in Upper Cretaceous rocks in Montana. Every bone seems to be a bird bone, every joint a bird joint. It was no doubt a warm-blooded animal that was covered with feathers.

A RANGE OF DROMAEOSAURIDS

About the size of a goose, *Bambiraptor* is the smallest dromaeosaurid. Turkey-sized *Velociraptor* is probably the best known. Scientists were first alerted to the birdlike nature of these animals in the 1960s, when tiger-sized *Deinonychus* was discovered. Bigger dromaeosaurids are only known from fragments of bone. *Utahraptor* probably weighed more than a ton, while *Megaraptor* (not shown), known only from a 13-inch (34-cm) killing claw, must have approached the size of the big meat eaters, such as *Allosaurus* (*see pages 18–19*). Most of these animals were found in Upper Cretaceous rocks in North America.

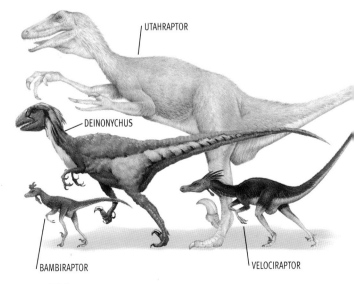

UTAHRAPTOR

DEINONYCHUS

BAMBIRAPTOR

VELOCIRAPTOR

EGGS & NESTS

Like modern birds, some dinosaurs built nests and laid eggs. The first known
dinosaur nests were found by an expedition sent to the Gobi Desert from the
American Museum of Natural History in 1923. The nests were among remains of
herds of the horned dinosaur *Protoceratops*. Alongside the supposed *Protoceratops*
eggs lay the skeleton of a toothless meat eater, *Oviraptor*. This so-called "egg
thief" was thought to have been buried in a sandstorm while digging up the eggs.
As sometimes happens, however, more evidence caused later paleontologists to
re-evaluate this interpretation. In the 1990s, another expedition to the Gobi Desert
found the fossil of an *Oviraptor* sitting on a nest, incubating eggs, which meant
those first nests must also have been *Oviraptor* nests!

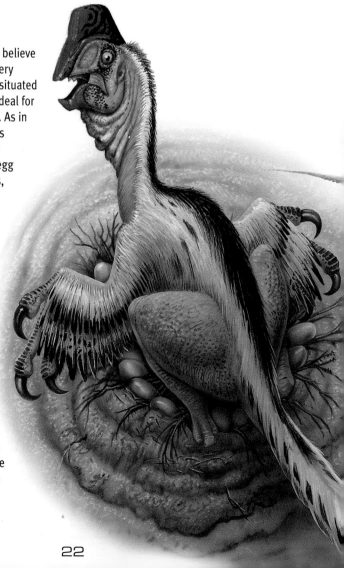

OVIRAPTOR HEAD

An *Oviraptor's* head makes it easy to believe
it might have been an egg eater. Its very
short, beaklike mouth and its gullet, situated
over the widest part of its jaw, were ideal for
swallowing something big and round. As in
modern egg-eating snakes, two bones
protruding down from its palate were
perfectly positioned to tear open an egg
on its way down. With its long fingers,
which were just right for grasping
eggs, *Oviraptor* may have been an
egg-eating dinosaur after all. There
seems to have been little else for
it to eat on the desert plains of
Late Cretaceous Mongolia.

NESTING
DINOSAUR

In the 1990s, a fossil of an
Oviraptor was found sitting on
a nest with its arms spread
protectively around some eggs,
evidently keeping them warm with its
body heat. Modern birds do this, since
their feathers provide insulation. This
is one piece of evidence suggesting
that *Oviraptor*, and many other
birdlike dinosaurs, had feathers.

TROODON EGGS

Fossils of *Troodon* nests show they were oval ridges of mud surrounding the eggs, very much like the nests of *Oviraptor*. The eggs were laid in pairs, which suggests that the dinosaur had a pair of oviducts (egg tubes) within its body. A modern bird has only one oviduct. Birds have evolved many such features, which keep down their body weight to make flying easier.

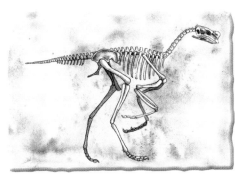

EGG THIEF

The jaw of *Caenagnathus* was similar to that of *Chirostenotes*, a turkey-sized dinosaur with very long fingers that would have enabled it to pick up mollusks and insects or raid other dinosaur nests for their eggs. Perhaps there were many different kinds of egg-stealing dinosaurs in Late Cretaceous times.

CAENAGNATHUS JAWBONE

Caenagnathus was a dinosaur that probably resembled *Oviraptor* and may have been an egg eater. Certainly, its toothless lower jaw was quite wide in the middle and would have been good for swallowing eggs. As no other remains have been found, *Caenagnathus* remains a bit of a mystery.

TROODON

Troodon was one of the maniraptorans, although it was not quite as birdlike as the dromaeosaurids. This small meat eater of the late Cretaceous Period was about 8 feet (2.5 m) long and may well have had feathers.

TRIASSIC 248-206 MYA	EARLY/MID JURASSIC 206-159 MYA	LATE JURASSIC 159-144 MYA	EARLY CRETACEOUS 144-97 MYA	LATE CRETACEOUS 97-65 MYA

23

BIRD OR DINOSAUR?

As well as finding the first dinosaur nests, the U.S. expeditions to
the Gobi Desert in the 1920s uncovered many other dinosaur remains. One
of these that we now call *Mononykus* was a total puzzle. Was it a bird or was it a
dinosaur? If it was a bird, its arms were too short for it to fly. If it was a dinosaur,
what good were hands reduced to a single finger with a big claw? In the 1980s,
when new specimens were discovered, *Mononykus* was found to have belonged
to a group of related animals, the alvarezsaurids—a distinct group within the
maniraptorans—that ranged from South America to Central Asia. Today, we still
do not know whether they were birds or dinosaurs.

A HALFWAY STAGE

All sorts of other animals seem to have been
intermediate in the evolution from dinosaurs to
birds. The size of an ostrich, *Unenlagia* was far
too big to fly, even though its arms were in the
form of small wings. Perhaps these wings
helped the animal balance and provided
direction control as it ran across open plains.
Whatever their function, they probably
evolved from the working wings of an
ancestor that did fly.

RHEA

A modern rhea, the running bird of today's
Argentinian plains, uses its stumpy wings to steer
itself while running. Modern flightless birds have
evolved from flying ancestors, just as the
maniraptorans probably did back in the age of dinosaurs.

TRIASSIC 248-206 MYA	EARLY/MID JURASSIC 206-159 MYA	LATE JURASSIC 159-144 MYA	EARLY CRETACEOUS 144-97 MYA	LATE CRETACEOUS 97-65 MYA

OSTRICH

One function of non-flying wings in modern running birds is for display. The ostrich makes a big show of its wing feathers when it is courting a mate or threatening an enemy. It is quite possible that the part-bird/part-dinosaur animals of the Cretaceous Period also had flamboyant feathers on their flightless wings and used them for display. Unfortunately, such behavior cannot be proven by fossil evidence.

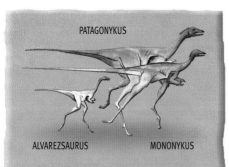

PATAGONYKUS

ALVAREZSAURUS   MONONYKUS

THREE ALVAREZSAURIDS

The first alvarezsaurid to be described was *Alvarezsaurus* itself, found in Argentina in the 1970s. This specimen had no forelimbs, so it did not look too unusual, but it did have a very birdlike body. In the early 1990s, good specimens of *Mononykus* were found in Mongolia, and scientists realized these were two very similar animals. In 1991, again in Argentina, the discovery of *Patagonykus* confirmed that there were several related animals in the alvarezsaurid group.

MONONYKUS

The best known and most complete of the alvarezsaurids was *Mononykus*. It looked like a very lightly built, meat-eating dinosaur with spindly legs and a long tail. The two forelimbs are remarkable. They are short and have a shelf of bone, which in modern birds would support wing feathers, and each bears a single stout, stubby claw. These forelimbs probably evolved from the functional wings of a flying ancestor, such as the Late Jurassic *Archaeopteryx*.

BIRD MIMICS

One group of dinosaurs has always been thought to look very much like birds. Ornithomimids ("bird mimics") had plump, compact bodies; big eyes; toothless beaks on small heads that were supported on long, slender necks; and long legs with thick muscles close to the hip. Typical of the group was *Struthiomimus* ("ostrich mimic") from the Late Cretaceous. Although they fall into the category of meat-eating dinosaurs and would have descended from purely carnivorous ancestors, these dinosaurs were probably omnivorous, eating fruit and leaves as well as insects and small vertebrates, such as lizards. Ostriches and other ground birds of today are also omnivores.

EMU

A modern emu is a plains-living animal. The keen eyes in the head, held high on top of a long neck, can spot danger from far across open spaces. Its strong running legs can take it out of danger at great speed. Because of the physical similarity, we think the Late Cretaceous ornithomimids had a similar life on the plains of North America and central Asia.

GALLIMIMUS

GARIDUMIMUS

ORNITHOMIMIDS

All ornithomimids looked similar but varied somewhat in size. *Struthiomimus* was about the size of an ostrich. *Pelecanimimus* was one of the earliest. It had a pouch of skin beneath its long jaws, which had hundreds of tiny teeth. This suggests that the teeth of the group became smaller and smaller before disappearing altogether in the later ornithomimids. *Garidumimus*, named after a mythical Hindu bird, had a small crest on its head. The biggest known was *Gallimimus,* the "chicken mimic" at 13–16 feet (4–5 m) long. Some chicken!

PELECANIMIMUS

TRIASSIC 248-206 MYA	EARLY/MID JURASSIC 206-159 MYA	LATE JURASSIC 159-144 MYA	EARLY CRETACEOUS 144-97 MYA	LATE CRETACEOUS 97-65 MYA

GALLIMIMUS SKELETON

Gallimimus, probably the best known of the ornithomimids, had a small, toothless beak. This dinosaur was built for speed and could run at up to 50 miles (80 km) per hour, as fast as a race horse. It usually paced around slowly, stalking small mammals or snapping up seeds and insects, but its speed meant that it could escape from most predators. Its long tail acted as a counterbalance to the front of the body, propelling it forward while it sprinted. Its hipbone also pointed forward. This skeleton is on display at the Natural History Museum in London.

TERRIBLE HAND

An intriguing fossil from Late Cretaceous rocks in Mongolia shows a pair of arms, 8 feet (2.5 m) long, with three-clawed hands. The animal has been given the name *Deinocheirus*, but we know nothing else about it. The bones look as if they are from an ornithomimid, but they are far bigger than those of any known member of this group. For now, the owner of these extraordinary bones remains a mystery.

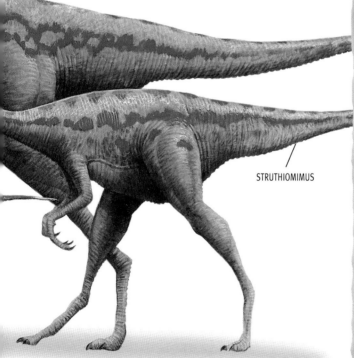

STRUTHIOMIMUS

BUILT FOR SPEED

As with most meat-eating dinosaurs, the skeleton of an ornithomimid, such as this *Ornithomimus*, is very birdlike. Balanced by its long tail, its head would have been held farther forward than that of an ostrich. However, it had very similar legs, with a very short femur (thighbone) that would have held all the muscles so the lower leg and the toes were worked only by tendons. This gives a very lightweight leg that could move quickly— a good running leg.

SEGNOSAURIDS

Sometimes, part of a skeleton is so unlike any known dinosaur that nobody knows what kind it is. Such is the case with segnosaurids. In the 1920s, the first bones, found in Upper Cretaceous rocks in Mongolia, were thought to be from a giant turtle, but they were reclassified as dinosaur remains in the 1970s. The various bits of bone were so unalike that they seemed to be from different families of dinosaur. Even now, the name therizinosaurid is sometimes used for the group. This name was first used as the original classification of the forelimb, as opposed to segnosaurid, the name chosen when the skull and backbone were studied. These dinosaurs were classified as meat eaters, then as prosauropods, one of the long-necked plant eaters. For the time being, at least, they are back with the meat eaters.

SEGNOSAURUS

Typical of the group, *Segnosaurus* had a relatively small head and a heavy body supported on short hind legs. Its curved backbone must have given it a stooped appearance. Perhaps its most surprising feature is the presence of enormous, sickle-like talons on its hands. One segnosaurid, *Beipiaosaurus* (discovered in 1999), had the remains of fine, featherlike structures around its limbs. At 6.5 feet (2 m) long, it is the biggest known feathered dinosaur. Like some of the more birdlike dinosaurs, segnosaurids seem to have been covered with some kind of plumage.

A MODERN PARALLEL

The anteater is a modern animal with claws that seem too big for its body. It uses them to rip through the tough walls of anthills to get at the ant colony. Some scientists have suggested that this is how segnosaurids lived.

TRIASSIC	EARLY/MID JURASSIC	LATE JURASSIC	EARLY CRETACEOUS	LATE CRETACEOUS
248-206 MYA	206-159 MYA	159-144 MYA	144-97 MYA	97-65 MYA

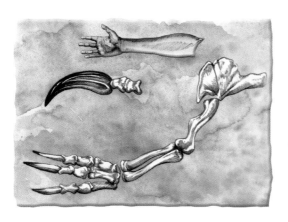

MIGHTY CLAWS

The forearms of *Therizinosaurus* were almost as long as those of the mysterious *Deinocheirus* (*see page 27*). However, much of their length consisted of the fingers, one of which had a claw that measured 2.5 feet (70 cm) long. That was just the length of the bone of the claw. With the horny sheath on it, the claw would have been half as long again. How could this claw have been used? Paleontologists are still guessing today.

ERLIKOSAURUS SKULL

The only known segnosaurid skull is that of *Erlikosaurus*. It looks very much like the skulls of some of the big plant-eating dinosaurs. Behind its toothless beak, the teeth are small and leaf shaped. Some scientists have suggested that this might be the skull of a fish-eating dinosaur and that the foot bones (which are also unusual) could have been webbed for swimming. However, the rest of the skeleton suggests that it could not have been a swimming animal.

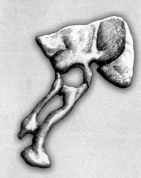

SEGNOSAURUS HIPBONE

The hipbones of meat-eating dinosaurs are usually distinctive. The pubis bone at the front points forward. In the segnosaurids, however, this bone sweeps backward. This is usually only seen in plant-eating dinosaurs, as it gives more space for the big plant-eating intestines that such animals need. Such a pubis bone would have given a segnosaurid's body a very dumpy appearance. This is part of what makes the whole group a puzzle.

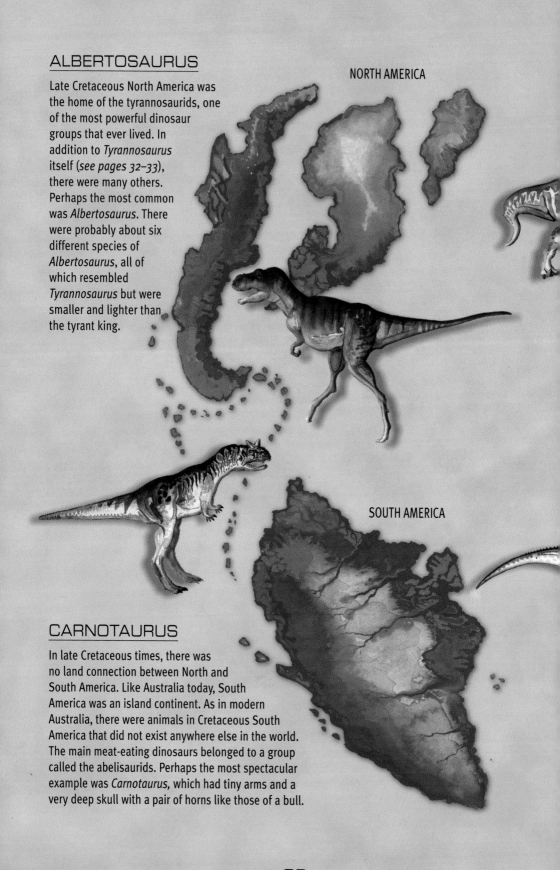

ALBERTOSAURUS

Late Cretaceous North America was the home of the tyrannosaurids, one of the most powerful dinosaur groups that ever lived. In addition to *Tyrannosaurus* itself (*see pages 32–33*), there were many others. Perhaps the most common was *Albertosaurus*. There were probably about six different species of *Albertosaurus*, all of which resembled *Tyrannosaurus* but were smaller and lighter than the tyrant king.

NORTH AMERICA

SOUTH AMERICA

CARNOTAURUS

In late Cretaceous times, there was no land connection between North and South America. Like Australia today, South America was an island continent. As in modern Australia, there were animals in Cretaceous South America that did not exist anywhere else in the world. The main meat-eating dinosaurs belonged to a group called the abelisaurids. Perhaps the most spectacular example was *Carnotaurus*, which had tiny arms and a very deep skull with a pair of horns like those of a bull.

LATE CRETACEOUS ISOLATION

EUROPE

ASIA

Early in the dinosaur age, all continents of the world were part of Pangaea, a single supercontinent (see page 10). It took 150 million years for Pangaea to break up into the continents we know today. At the start of the dinosaur age, the same kinds of dinosaurs lived all over the world. But Earth's surface was splitting apart as rift valleys opened up and formed seas and oceans. Animals then evolved in different ways. By the end of the Mesozic, meat eaters still lived on each continent but were no longer closely related to those on other landmasses.

ASIA'S TYRANNOSAURIDS

The Bering Strait probably did not exist at the start of the age of dinosaurs. North America was joined to Asia by a broad neck of land extending from Alaska, and similar animals lived on both continents. The main big meat eaters in Asia were also tyrannosaurids. *Albertosaurus* did not reach into Asia. Instead, Asia supported tyrannosaurids of its own.

AFRICA

MADAGASCAR

DELTADROMEUS

On the continent of Africa, the biggest of the meat-eaters (*see Carcharodontosaurus, page 35*) were evolved from animals that resembled *Allosaurus* (*see pages 18–19*). However, there were a number of others, such as *Deltadromeus,* that had evolved from the small meat eaters— the coelurosaurids—of Jurassic times.

MAJUNGASAURUS

The big meat-eating dinosaur found on the island of Madagascar was *Majungatholus*. It is interesting that it was an abelisaurid, like the meat eaters of South America and India. This means that before the continents split up, South America, Madagascar, and India were joined together long enough for abelisaurids' ancestors to migrate across all three continents while they were still attached to Antarctica and after Africa had drifted away (abelisaurids are not commonly found in Africa).

TRIASSIC 245-208 MYA	EARLY/MID JURASSIC 208-157 MYA	LATE JURASSIC 157-146 MYA	EARLY CRETACEOUS 146-97 MYA	LATE CRETACEOUS 97-65 MYA

TYRANNOSAURIDS

At 39 feet (12 m) long and 20 feet (6 m) tall, *Tyrannosaurus* must have been the scourge of the North American continent at the end of the dinosaur age. So far, about 15 specimens of *Tyrannosaurus* have been discovered in various states of completeness. From these we have a picture of what the mighty beasts looked like. However, there is still much debate about how they lived. Some scientists think they actively hunted, perhaps waiting in ambush for duckbills, the big plant eaters of the time, then charging out at them from the cover of the forest. Others insist they were too big for such activity but would have scavenged carrion, the meat of already-dead animals. Maybe they did both.

A RANGE OF TYRANNOSAURIDS

Daspletosaurus from North America was similar to *Tyrannosaurus* but was a little smaller and had a heavy head with fewer but larger teeth. At about 20 feet (6 m) long, *Alioramus* was a medium-sized tyrannosaurid from Asia. It had a long skull with knobbles and spikes along the top. The smallest was *Nanotyrannus*, from Montana, at 13 feet (4 m) long. Experts are undecided about this last one. Some think it may have been a small *Albertosaurus*.

TYRANT LIZARD KING

Tyrannosaurus, the biggest of the tyrannosaurids, is often known by its full species name *Tyrannosaurus rex* or simply *T. rex*. Other dinosaurs also have full species names, such as *Allosaurus atrox*, *Velociraptor mongoliensis*, and so on, but these are usually only used by scientists.

COPROLITE

Fossilized animal droppings are known to geologists as coprolites, and they give useful clues to an extinct animal's diet. As with footprints, however, it is often impossible to tell what animal made which coprolite. Big coprolites, more than 8 inches (20 cm) long, that may have come from *Tyrannosaurus*, have been found to contain smashed, undigested bone fragments.

FOOTPRINT

In the late 1980s, a dinosaur footprint almost 3 feet (1 m) long was discovered on a slab of Upper Cretaceous rock in New Mexico. Whatever beast made the print had the claws of a meat eater. There was only one print, so the stride of the animal must have been greater than the almost 10-foot- (3-m-) long slab of rock. Scientists say the animal was moving at 5–6 miles (8–10 km) per hour. We cannot be sure this footprint was made by *Tyrannosaurus*, but we know of no bigger meat-eating dinosaurs in Cretaceous America.

FRIGHTFUL BITE

Tyrannosaurus had incredibly powerful jaws and teeth used to rip flesh from its prey. Gouges in the pelvic bone of a Late Cretaceous specimen of the three-horned dinosaur *Triceratops* exactly match the size and spacing of the teeth of *Tyrannosaurus*. From these marks, scientists could tell that a *Tyrannosaurus* bit down into the meat of the hind leg and tore it away from the bone when the *Triceratops* was already dead. But whether it was the *Tyrannosaurus* that killed it, nobody can tell.

DASPLETOSAURUS

ALIORAMUS

NANOTYRANNUS

TRIASSIC 248-206 MYA	EARLY/MID JURASSIC 206-159 MYA	LATE JURASSIC 159-144 MYA	EARLY CRETACEOUS 144-97 MYA	LATE CRETACEOUS 97-65 MYA

THE NEW KINGS

What was the biggest, strongest, and fiercest meat-eating dinosaur that ever lived? *Tyrannosaurus*? Not any more! For the past hundred years we have said that *Tyrannosaurus* was the most powerful of the meat-eating dinosaurs. Generations of scientists have believed this to be so and have even stated that it would be mechanically impossible for bigger meat-eating animals to have existed. But now, the remains of even bigger meat eaters are being found. In the 1990s, the skeletons of two carnivorous dinosaurs were found within a year of one another: one in South America, the other in Africa. Although neither skeleton was complete, they appear to have belonged to a group of dinosaurs that were even longer than *Tyrannosaurus*.

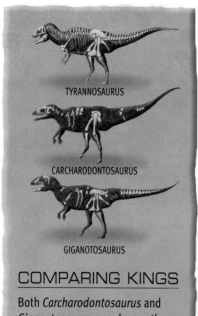

TYRANNOSAURUS

CARCHARODONTOSAURUS

GIGANOTOSAURUS

COMPARING KINGS

Both *Carcharodontosaurus* and *Giganotosaurus* were longer than the previous record-holder, *Tyrannosaurus*. As shown above, however, only *Tyrannosaurus* is known from complete skeletons, and there is still a lot we don't know about the other two. Even so, *Tyrannosaurus* seems to have been a much heavier animal and was higher at the hip, so we could still say that the biggest meat-eating dinosaur that is completely known is *Tyrannosaurus*. Still the king!

GIGANOTOSAURUS

The great meat-eating dinosaur *Giganotosaurus* seems to have been closely related to *Carcharodontosaurus*, even though it lived in isolated South America in the Late Cretaceous Period, while the other lived in Africa. It is likely that in the early part of the Cretaceous Period, before the continents were separated by oceans, the ancestors of these animals spread across the whole world. After the continents split apart, *Giganotosaurus* began to evolve separately.

MONSTROUS SKULL

The skull of *Carcharodontosaurus* is almost completely known. When putting the skull bones together, the scientists only had to recreate the missing front of the snout and the bones at the very rear. This they could do by drawing on their knowledge of other skulls. The final skull is 5 feet (1.5 m) long and has strong, curved, shark-like teeth. We know far less about the skull of *Giganotosaurus*. What we can be sure of is that the jaws were not as powerful as those of *Tyrannosaurus*, the teeth were not as strong, and it had an even smaller brain than the Tyrant Lizard King.

CARCHARODONTOSAURUS

Related to the Jurassic *Allosaurus* (*see pages 18–19*), *Carcharodontosaurus* came from Morocco, in North Africa. Some fossils of this creature were discovered by a German expedition in 1925, but they were destroyed when their museum was bombed during World War II, along with the original remains of *Spinosaurus* found on the same expedition. Only when more fossils were discovered in the mid-1990s did paleontologists realize that *Carcharodontosaurus* was a 50-foot- (15-m-) long giant.

TRIASSIC 248-206 MYA	EARLY/MID JURASSIC 206-159 MYA	LATE JURASSIC 159-144 MYA	EARLY CRETACEOUS 144-97 MYA	LATE CRETACEOUS 97-65 MYA

DID YOU KNOW?

The first dinosaurs were meat eaters.

The smallest known dinosaurs were all meat eaters.

Dinosaurs can be named after all sorts of things:

Gojirasaurus—a large early meat-eater—from the Japanese movie monster *Godzilla*.

Borogovia—a relative of *Troodon*—from a mythical animal in a Lewis Carroll poem.

Carcharodontosaurus—(*see page 35*)–after the great white shark.

Gasosaurus—a tiger-sized hunter—from the gas company that financed its excavation.

Irritator—(*see page 15*)—after the frustration caused to palaeontologists after the finder had tampered with the fossil.

Garudimimus–after a local deity in the area in which it was found.

Bambiraptor–(*see page 21*)—despite being named after a gentle cartoon character, this was a vicious little beast.

Not all of the carnivorous dinosaur group—the theropods—ate meat. *Incisivosaurus*, a relative of *Oviraptor* (*see page 22*) had rabbit-like teeth at the front of its mouth and plant-grinding teeth at the back. The whole segnosaur group (*see pages 28–29*) was probably vegetarian.

It is said that the maniraptorans like *Velociraptor* (*see page 21*) were the smartest dinosaurs—almost as smart as some of today's birds. In fact they were about as smart as emus— the dumbest of today's birds.

There were far fewer carnivorous dinosaurs than plant-eating ones. Just like nowadays there are far fewer lions than wildebeest on the African plains.

Of over 500 species of dinosaur known, about a fifth of them are meat eaters.

The basic shape of a meat-eating dinosaur—long jaws with sharp teeth, long body, hands with three claws or less, strong hind legs balanced by a heavy tail—was established at the beginning of the age of dinosaurs. The result is a swiftly moving animal with the killing apparatus, the teeth and the claws, held out at the front. All meat-eating dinosaurs are based on a shape like this.

Mei long, a little relative of *Troodon* (p.18), was found curled up with its head tucked under its arm, the way a bird sleeps. Its name means "soundly sleeping dragon."

The birds evolved from the meat-eating dinosaurs, and some of the early types are so dinosaur-like that it is almost impossible to tell whether they are birds or dinosaurs. In fact some palaeontologists regard birds as part of the dinosaur group, referring to the others as "non-avian dinosaurs."

Tyrannosaurus **did not roar.** Analysis of the skull shows that it probably croaked like a bullfrog.

When a slab of rock containing a small fossil is split in two, the fossil may be embedded in one side of the split or the other. Otherwise, parts of the fossil may be embedded in both. Palaeontologists give this occurrence the term "part and counterpart." Both are important in the study of the fossil. But this can lead to confusion. Unscrupulous fossil collectors may sell it as two separate fossils. The two parts can be given different names by different scientists, unaware of what has happened.

Because of the long tail we used to think that a meat-eating dinosaur sat upright like a kangaroo, using the tail as a prop. Now we know that it used the tail for balancing, like a tightrope-walker's pole.

The teeth can tell us what a dinosaur ate. The many closely-spaced teeth of *Baryonyx* (*see page 15*) are those of a fish-eater. *Tyrannosaurus* (*see page 32*) had short stout teeth at the front for holding struggling prey, and blade-like teeth at the side for shearing through the flesh of large animals.

Not all tyrannosaurs were big brutes. Their earliest ancestors, such as *Stokesosaurus*, from the late Jurassic of Utah and England, was a feathered emu-sized animal.

Carnivorous dinosaur teeth kept being replaced. As they became worn and dropped out, a new one was already in the socket to take its place. There were, in fact, several at different stages of growth in each socket at the same time.

Sometimes big dinosaurs became trapped in muddy river beds. This provided a great source of easy food for carnivores. Unfortunately for them, many became trapped themselves, and we find their remains fossilized along with their proposed meal. Palaeontologists call this kind of occurrence a "predator trap."

SUMMARY TIMELINE

EORAPTOR

Coelophysis
Gojirasaurus
Herrerasaurus
Eoraptor
Earliest dinosaurs

**TRIASSIC/JURASSIC
BOUNDARY**

Gasosaurus
Megalosaurus
Eustreptospondylus
Monolophosaurus

**MIDDLE/UPPER
JURASSIC
BOUNDARY**

200

161

300

251

**BEGINNING OF
TRIASSIC
PERIOD**

175

**LOWER/
MIDDLE
JURASSIC
BOUNDARY**

Dilophosaurus
Megapnosaurus

MEGAPNOSAURUS

Scipionyx
Irritator
Deinonychus
Falcarius
Suchomimus
Smallest footpirnts
Utahraptor
Pelecanimimus
Incisivosaurus
Mei
Sinosauropteryx
Baryonyx

**LOWER/UPPER
CRETACEOUS
BOUNDARY**

99

BARYONYX

145
**JURASSIC/
CRETACEOUS
BOUNDARY**

100

65
**END OF
CRETACEOUS
PERIOD**

0
million
years ago

Nqwebasaurus	Tyrannosaurus	Alioramus
Haplocheirus	Nanotyrannus	Daspletosaurus
Allosaurus	Ornithomimus	Rahonavis
Compsognathus	Struthiomimus	Bambiraptor
Ceratosaurus	Gallimimus	Velociraptor
	Garudimimus	Mononykus
	Borogovia	Therizinosaurus
	Unenlagia	Oviraptor
	Patagonykus	Aerosteon
	Troodon	Caenagnathus
	Albertosaurus	Chirostenotes
	Albertonykus	Erlikosaurus
	Tarbosaurus	Segnosaurus
	Carnotaurus	Alvareszsasurus
	Majungasaurus	Gigantoraptor
	Austroraptor	Mapusaurus
		Giganotosaurus
		Spinosaurus
		Carcharodontosaurus

ALLOSAURUS

TROODON

WHERE DID THEY LIVE?

Carnivorous dinosaurs have been found all over the world, from *Cryolophosaurus* in Antarctica to a tyrannosaur in the northern tip of Baffin Island, eastwards from *Troodon* on Alaska's North Slope right across the continents to *Futabusaurus*, another tyrannosaur, in Japan.

But of course, even though they lived on every continent, we would only expect to find their remains in particular areas. They would only lie in areas in which there are rocks that were formed at the time the dinosaurs lived and died. Sedimentary rocks—those in which we find fossils—are formed where mud settles on shallow sea beds, or sands build up in river deltas, or clays gather at the bottom of lakes. In these places, if a dinosaur dies, then its body may be buried quickly and preserved to some extent. However, that is not the end of the story. After they are formed, the rocks and all the fossils in them may be destroyed by mountain building or weathering. So dinosaur remains are very rare indeed.

In North America dinosaur discoveries form quite complex patterns, depending on the geology and the mountain-building history. Sedimentary rocks that formed at the end of the Triassic period—the time of the earliest dinosaurs—outcrop in areas as far apart as Arizona and Massachusetts. River deposits from ancient oases in Arizona and desert sandstones in Massachusetts reveal the bones of small meat-eating dinosaurs such as *Coelophysis*. There were no big meat-eating dinosaurs at that time. Because all the continents were jammed together into one single supercontinent in the Triassic period, *Coelophysis* and other small Triassic dinosaurs like them, have been found in rocks dating from that time in South Africa and Germany.

The arid environments that gave rise to the desert and oasis conditions of the late Triassic continued into the early Jurassic, and we find the same kinds of dinosaur remains in the same places—the south-western states and the eastern seaboard.

In the late Jurassic period, the heyday of the dinosaurs, much of the mid-west was covered by an inland sea which gradually dried out and was replaced by river plains. Here we have the most famous remains of Jurassic dinosaur fossils in a sequence of rocks called the Morrison Formation that stretches from New Mexico northward, well into Canada. The plant-eating dinosaurs of this area were preyed upon by small meat eaters such as *Ornitholestes*, medium-sized ones like *Stokesosaurus*, and big ones like *Allosaurus*.

Lake beds and quiet lagoons make the best types of rock for preserving small dinosaurs. Thinly-bedded mudstones from the early Cretaceous in China have thrown up all sorts of tiny dinosaurs, some of which are covered in feathers and look very similar to birds. One, *Microraptor*, was so small and light that it could glide from tree to tree on gliding wings formed from feathers on both front and hind legs. Yes! It had four wings! Before its discovery the smallest dinosaur known was *Compsognathus*, found in fine late Jurassic limestones that were deposited on the bottom of a quiet lagoon in Germany.

Come the end of dinosaur times, at the end of the Cretaceous period, the continents had broken apart and were spread across the globe. Different animals were found on different landmasses. In North America it was the rule of the tyrannosaurs, with *Tyrannosaurus* itself being the biggest carnivore of the time. Its remains are mostly found in the northern states of the mid-west, particularly South Dakota and Montana, but they have also been found from Texas to Alberta.

However, the distribution of these discoveries does not necessarily mean that that is the only places where the dinosaurs lived. Those that lived in upland areas would not have been fossilized, as they were too far away from places where rocks were forming. In fact a tyrannosaur, called *Appalachiosaurus*, has been found in Alabama—a long, long way from the accepted tyrannosaur stomping ground.

And, of course, we only know the dinosaurs whose remains lie close to the surface. There must be many more lying deep within the earth, buried too deeply ever to be reached by paleontologists.

NEW DISCOVERIES

Paleontology as a science never stands still. Every year, every month, every week even, something new is found out about dinosaurs. It is estimated that between 10 and 20 new dinosaur species are being found each year. As a result, sadly a book such as this will be a little out of date before it gets on to the shelves. Here are a few of the newest discoveries made in the past few years.

A new study of *Sinosauropteryx*, closely related to *Compsognathus* (*see page 16*), found in China showed not only its feathers but also its color. It had a Mohican-like crest of bristly feathers running along the top of its head and down the middle of its back, as well as an overall insulating coat. The color-bearing cells in the feathers show that its tail was striped orange and white in life.

Although *Sinosauropteryx* was feathered, there is evidence that *Compsognathus* had naked lizard-like skin.

There is now a specimen of the ancestor of the strange alvarezsaurids (*see pages 24–25*). *Haplocheirus* was almost identical to the others of the alvarezsaurid group, but lived in the late Jurassic, about 15 million years before the others. It had not yet evolved the unusual forelimbs but the conventional three fingers on the hand. However the arm muscles were very strong—a good basis for the evolution of the stocky, single-fingered forelimb of the later species.

Aerosteon, an elephant-sized meat eater recently found in South America and related to *Giganotosaurus* (*see page 34*), seems to have breathed like a bird. Instead of expanding and contracting lungs like we would expect, it seems to have had quite rigid lungs that fed expandable sacs that drew the air in and out. Hollows in the bones show this—in fact the name means "airy bone." Such a system would have given the animal lots of energy and shows that it must have been a very active hunter.

New studies of the skeleton of *Velociraptor* (*see page 21*) show that it had this kind of breathing system as well.

Sinornithosaurus, a turkey-sized carnivorous dinosaur, one of the most famous of the feathered dinosaurs from China, had a poisonous bite. Although the skeleton had been known for about ten years nobody noticed that it had cavities in the jaw that would have contained poison sacs, and grooves in the teeth for channeling the poison, as in some modern poisonous snakes. It could be that the poison was used for subduing the birds on which it fed.

Albertonykus is currently America's smallest dinosaur. It was an alvarezsaurid (*see pages 24–25*), about the size of a chicken and lived in the late Cretaceous. We now know much more about the growth rate of *Tyrannosaurus* (*see page 34*) than we once did. It seems that they grew slowly at first, taking about 14 years to reach a length of 7 feet (2.1 m). Then they put on a spurt of growth and by 18 years old they were about 22 feet (2.7 m)long. Thereafter, they continued to grow slowly until reaching a maximum length of about 40 feet (12.1 m), and died after about 30 years.

The earliest segnosaurids (*see pages 28–29*) seem to have evolved in Utah. A whole graveyard of the primitive type *Falcarius* was found there, and their remains showed that they were beginning

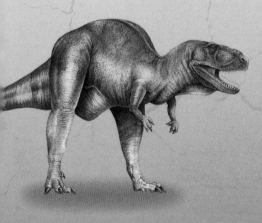

to evolve into plant eaters from meat-eating ancestors.

The group of giant meat eaters that include *Carcharodontosaurus* and *Giganotosaurus* (*see pages 34–35*) now has an even bigger member, *Mapusaurus*. Although complete skeletons have not been found, it had a skull that was more massive and a shin bone that was longer than its relative *Giganotosaurus*.

The biggest dromaeosaurid (*see pages 20–21*) known, 21-foot-long *Austroraptor*, has been discovered in Argentina. It probably hunted the big long-necked plant-eaters of the area.

A huge relative of *Oviraptor* (*see page 22*) has turned up in China. Called *Gigantoraptor*, it was 26 feet (8 m) long and twice the height of a man at the shoulder.

Dinosaurs did not have it all their own way. They were not the only hunters to be feared in the Mesozoic. We have now found the remains of an early Cretaceous badger-sized mammal *Repenomaus* in China that actually ate baby dinosaurs. There is also the remains of a twelve-foot-long (3.6 m) snake, *Sanajeh*, found in a late Cretaceous dinosaur nest in India, fossilized in the act of stealing the eggs.

MOVIES, WEBSITES, & FURTHER READING

MOVIES

Don't watch movies to get facts about dinosaurs! However, it is interesting to watch dinosaur movies to see how the view of dinosaurs has changed over the years. Here are some examples.

JURASSIC PARK (1993)
The most accurate depiction of movie dinosaurs up to that time, but the movie makers took the science and changed it to make it a more exciting story.

Tyrannosaurus (*see page 34*) The hips are the wrong shape and the head is too broad.

Velociraptor (*see page 21*) Made out to be too intelligent. Too big (but it was actually based on the larger *Deinonychus*). We now know that it was covered in feathers.

Dilophosaurus (*see page 12*) Too small, and showing a totally fictitious expandable frill and an ability to spit poison.

KING KONG (1933)
Again, the most accurate depiction of movie dinosaurs up to that time. Their design was based on the artwork of Charles R. Knight, one of the best dinosaur artists ever, and whose work is still on show in the American Museum of Natural History in New York, and the Field Museum in Chicago. It featured a *Tyrannosaurus*, that sat upright on its tail like a kangaroo (which it was thought to have done at the time). It also had the eye in the wrong position, and this was because it followed a painting in which Knight made the same mistake!

KING KONG (2005)
The movie makers did not even try to identify the dinosaurs shown here with any known species. Quite right! If dinosaurs still existed somewhere today, they would be unrecognizable—they would have continued to evolve over the past 65 million years.

THE ANIMAL WORLD (1956)
A wildlife documentary that featured a ten minute sequence from the age of dinosaurs. *Allosaurus* (*see pages 18–19*), *Ceratosaurus* (*see page 13*) and *Tyrannosaurus* (*see page 34*) all looked the same. That is because the models used came out of the same mould! All sitting up, tail dragging kangaroo style.

ONE MILLION YEARS B.C. (1966)
A fantasy that pitted cavemen against dinosaurs, but the dinosaurs were quite nicely sculpted.

Allosaurus (*see pages 18–19*). Head a bit too broad, and tail too flexible.

Ceratosaurus (*see page 13*). Whole animal too big, and again the tail too flexible.

An interesting point: in both these animals, and those in THE ANIMAL WORLD (done by the same sculptor/animator) the theropods' hands were held with the palms facing one another, not facing downward bunny style as was usually shown. We now know that theropods did hold their hands like this, but it did not become known until the 1980s.

WEBSITES

Wikipedia tends to be distrusted by many people because it is too easy to put spurious information on it. However, the dinosaur material published there is quite reliable and up to date.

www.dinosaursociety.com

All sorts of information on dinosaurs, including a valuable frequently updated page giving links to all the dinosaur-related news stories.

www.sciencedaily.com/news/fossils_ruins/ dinosaurs/

A catalog of the dinosaur stories run by this news site.

Warning! *The articles presented by these sites are usually written by journalists, not by dinosaur specialists. As a result they tend to be over-sensational or sometimes plain wrong. If you find an interesting dinosaur news story it is a good idea to chase it up through different sources, to see how the story differs. Usually you can tell how much is fact and how much has been made up by the reporter. That's fun, too!*

Google Earth

Key in DINOSAUR NATIONAL MONUMENT QUARRY VISITOR CENTER. This will take you to the site of one of the best public exposures of dinosaur remains. You can see little on the Google Earth image, except for the roof of the center, but if you pull back you can see the ridges of exposed rock running east-west (the "strike" in geological parlance) in which the dinosaur remains are found.

Key in HELL CREEK STATE PARK and see the kind of badlands landscape in which *Tyrannosaurus* is found.

Key in CLEVELAND LLOYD DINOSAUR QUARRY. The circular structure is the parking lot. Just to the north of it are two sheds. These cover the densest collection of Jurassic dinosaur fossils ever found. The remains of over 40 *Allosaurus* have been found there, probably trapped in a swamp while trying to eat plant-eating dinosaurs already trapped there (what we call a "predator trap").

FURTHER READING

THE DINOSAURIA

Edited by David B. Weishampel, Peter Dodson and Halszka Osmólska, 2nd edition 2004

This is the bible for paleontologists. However, it is extremely technical and hardly to be recommended for the casual reader. And, since the science is constantly changing, the 2nd edition may well be out of date already.

PREHISTORIC TIMES

A quarterly magazine, running since 1993, features articles on dinosaur research and dinosaur lore. See their website ***www.prehistorictimes.com***

GLOSSARY

Alvarezosaurid One of a group of small theropods with strong forelimbs carrying only a single claw.

Carboniferous The period of geological time from 359 to 299 million years ago. The time of the coal forests.

Carnivore An animal that eats meat.

Coelurosaurid One of a group of theropods distinguished by cavities in the tail bones. The coelurosaurs were once regarded as all small animals, but now we regard the great *Tyrannosaurus* as a member of the group.

Coprolite Fossil dung.

Crest A structure on the head of an animal, used for display. A crest may be made of bone, horn, or feathers.

Cretaceous The period of geological time from 145 to 65 million years ago. The last of the three dinosaur periods.

Digestive system The collection of organs in the body that processes food —the stomach, and intestines.

Dinosaur One of a group of reptiles that existed from the Triassic to the Cretaceous periods of Earth history.

Dromaeosaurid One of a group of small or medium-sized theropods that carried a killer claw on the foot.

Environment The total of all the surroundings in which an animal or a plant lives—the climate, the vegetation, the terrain, and so on.

Evolve To change from one type of animal to another over generations, in response to changing conditions.

Excavate To dig up.

Fossilize To turn to stone. An organism becomes fossilized when its organic material changes to mineral material after being buried for a long time in rock.

Jurassic The period of geological time between 199 and 145 million years ago. The heyday of the dinosaurs.

Juvenile An animal that has not reached its adult form.

Mammal A warm-blooded animal, usually covered in fur, that gives birth to live offspring and suckles its young.

Maniraptoran One of a group of small or medium-sized hunting theropods with strong grasping hands.

Omnivorous Able to eat both plants and animals.

Ornithomimid One of a group of medium-sized theropods with the outward appearance of an ostrich.

Paleontologist A scientist who studies paleontology.

Paleontology (spelled palaeontology in Europe). The study of the life of the past.

Pangaea The name given to the supercontinent that existed in Permian and Triassic times, that incorporated all the landmasses of the globe.

Pelvic bone One of the bones of the hip.

Permian The period of geological time from 299 to 251 million years ago. Reptiles were dominant on the land but the dinosaurs had not yet evolved.

Plumage The covering of feathers on a bird.

Rauisuchian One of a group of land-living hunting crocodiles that were the main hunters before the dinosaurs evolved.

Reptile A cold-blooded animal that reproduces by laying eggs, and is usually covered by a scaly skin. Lizards and snakes are typical modern reptiles.

Scavenger A carnivore that eats meat from animals that are already dead.

Skull The assemblage of bones in the skull.

Segnosaurid One of a group of medium- to large-sized theropods that were slow-moving and had adopted a plant-eating diet.

Spawning ground A particular area to which certain animals return to lay their eggs.

Spinosaurid One of a goup of large theropods, usually with fins on their backs and adaptations to fish-hunting.

Therizinosaurid An alternative name for a segnosaurid.

Theropod The group of dinosaurs to which all meat eaters belong.

Triassic The period of geological time between 151 and 199 million years ago, that saw the beginning of the age of dinosaurs.

INDEX

ACKNOWLEDGMENTS

The publishers would like to thank Helen Wire,
www.fossilfinds.com, and Elizabeth Wiggans for their assistance.

Picture Credits:
t=top, b=bottom, c=center, l=left, r=right

Lisa Alderson: 6bl, 6/7c, 14/15c, 21t, 24l, 25c, 29c, 35br. John Alston: 6tl, 10/11c,
11t, 16t, 16b, 18tl, 19t, 22cl, 22bl, 25tr, 28tl, 28bl, 29tr, 30/31, 32tl. Corbis: 10tl,
13b, 24b, 25tr, 27tr, 27br, 28cb. Dougal Dixon: 7b, 8b, 12b, 13tl, 13tr, 21b, 35tr.
Fossil Finds: 6cl, 16c, 23tr, 33br. Dr Peter Griffith: 19b, 22c. Simon Mendez:
10/11b, 12c, 14–15c, 20c, 21b, 23t, 24tl, 26/27c, 33cr, 34c, 36cr. Natural History
Museum: 11cr, 14tl, 33t. Oxford City Museum: 10b, 11b, 11tr. Planet Earth Pictures:
14bl. Luis Rey: 23c, 32/33c. Paul Sereno: 7cr, 34tr.

NOTE TO READERS
The website addresses are correct at the time of publishing. However, due to the ever-changing nature
of the Internet, websites and content may change. Some websites can contain links that are
unsuitable for children. The publisher is not responsible for changes in content or website
addresses. We advise that Internet searches should be supervised by an adult.

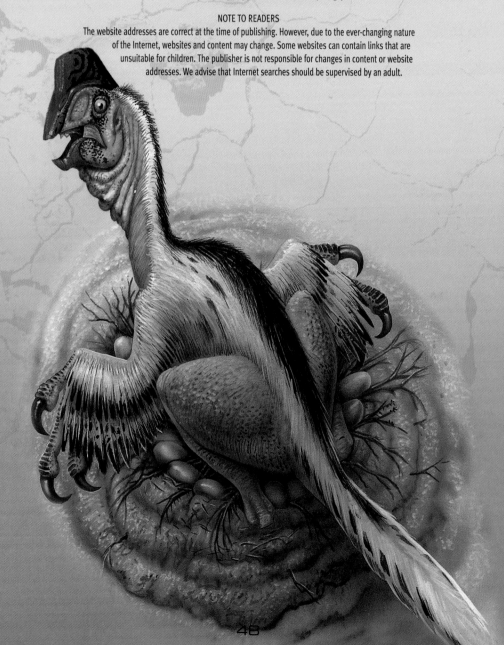